AMERICAN

HORSE

CAPTURING A PROUD SPIRIT

D. A. MICHAELS

KPT PUBLISHING

If you are not a horse person, it might be hard to understand why some people love their horses so much. There is something about the energy created that only comes from being on top of a horse. Whenever tense feelings come, one only needs to hop on for a short ride to realign priorities again—consider it cheap therapy.

It has been shown that the heartbeat of a horse can slow the human heartbeat, aiding in stress relief. Additionally, a horse's soft eyes can help calm a person, producing a sense of being loved, and can lead to feelings of value and purpose.

While this kind of experience is far from universal, there is verifiable evidence that spending time with a horse will bring a peace and calmness to a person's life. For the people who love horses, the time riding and caring for them is organic—although unspoken, the interactions are deep and fulfilling.

Luckily, you don't have to own a horse to spend time with a horse and reap some of the benefits. Horse stables nationwide accept volunteers as groundskeepers enthusiastically, offer riding classes, as well as trail rides. No matter your age, you will be amazed how just being around horses will bring satisfaction and fulfillment.

I hope you enjoy the book and can find a horse to love, and to love you.

D. A. MICHAELS

Horses are fast
Horses are free
Horses make me run
Horses make me dream

PAYTON WRIGHT
(4-year-old)

IF YOU HAVE SEEN NOTHING
BUT THE BEAUTY
OF THEIR MARKINGS AND LIMBS,
THEIR TRUE BEAUTY
IS HIDDEN FROM YOU.

There is something about
the gentle wisdom
in a horse's eye
that can put even
the most troubled soul
at peace.

Author Unknown

*I*n February 2017, my neighbor's husband suffered a fatal heart attack while attending his niece's wedding in Mexico, and although we were not close socially, we did help each other out now and then. When I heard of his sudden passing, the news hit me hard.

A widow myself, I live alone on an acreage with three horses, one dog, and two cats. I make it a point to talk to my kids every day to see how they are all doing. But if I don't answer the phone, no one automatically sends out a search party to see if I am all right. All at once it sank in: if I had a heart attack or got hurt in my pasture, nobody would look for me right away. Needless to say, I went into a bit of a funk—feeling vulnerable, slightly depressed, and a little scared.

I went out to the pasture to pet and talk to the horses because they are always willing to listen with no judgment. I had no halter or rope with me, but I walked up to my horse, Maverick, leaned against his neck with my fingers in his mane, and rested my head on his neck. Suddenly, he reached around and gave me a big hug with his head, so hard it actually hurt. When I wiggled away he straightened his head, then a minute later he gave me another big hug, and then another. He had never done anything like that before, nor has he done it since.

I admit, it brought tears to my eyes that somehow he knew that I needed a couple heartfelt hugs at that time. In fact, I still get tearful thinking about his extreme tenderness at that moment and how much I loved him for it. — JD

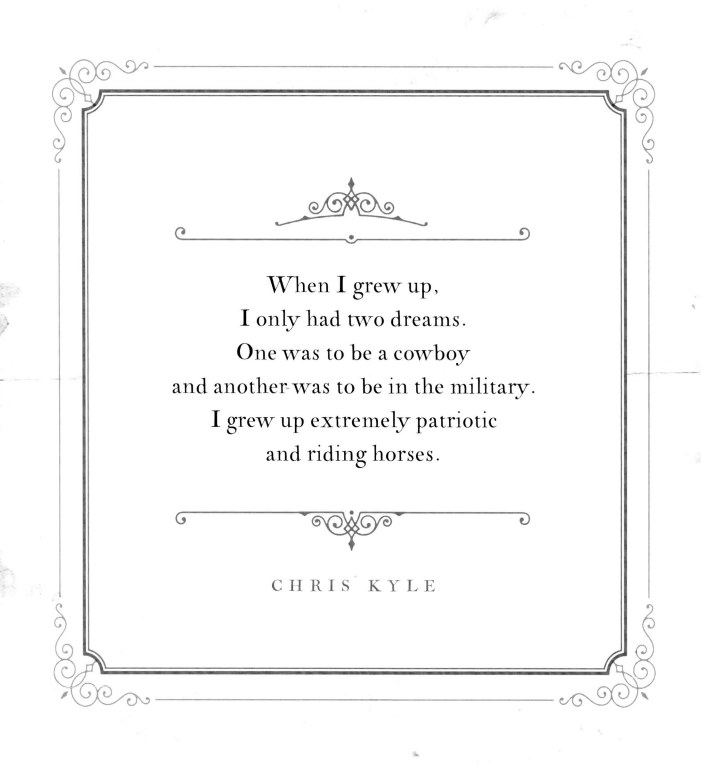

When I grew up,
I only had two dreams.
One was to be a cowboy
and another was to be in the military.
I grew up extremely patriotic
and riding horses.

CHRIS KYLE

The MAGNIFICENT HORSE

by Sue Ikerd

Beautiful creatures,
from Shetlands to Shires
Paintings and books
these equines inspire

There are sorrels and roans,
chestnut and bay
Palomino and buckskin,
Black, white and gray

They helped settle the West
and herded the cattle
Served in our wars,
carried generals into battle

Rode by commoners, kings,
and even Barbarians
Galloped across plains
by Native Americans

Horses cleared, plowed
and planted the land
And gathered the harvest
in partner with man

They pulled fancy rigs
and Romans in chariots
Bore jousting knights
and cowboys with lariats

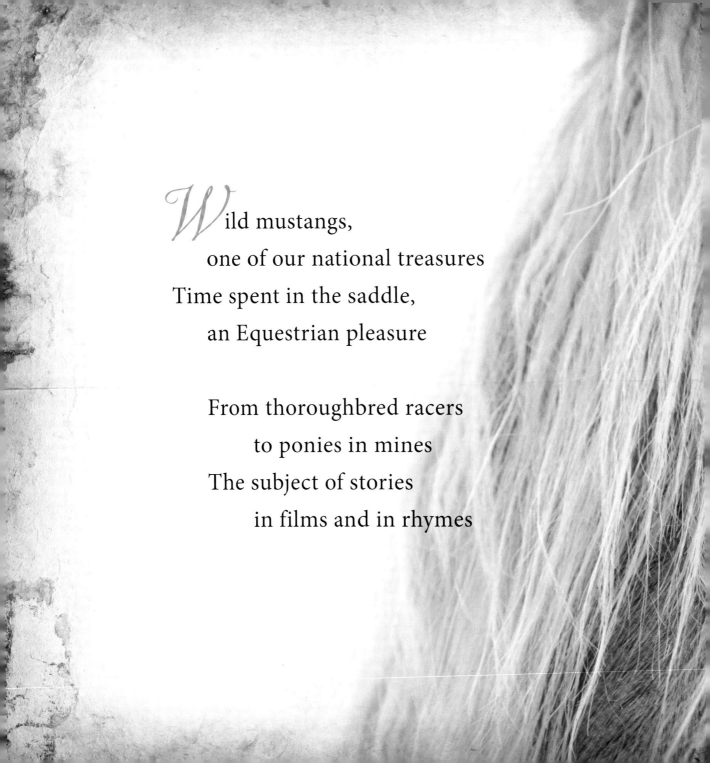

*W*ild mustangs,
  one of our national treasures
Time spent in the saddle,
  an Equestrian pleasure

  From thoroughbred racers
    to ponies in mines
  The subject of stories
    in films and in rhymes

*T*hroughout time
    they've been a remarkable force
God's versatile gift,
    the magnificent horse.

To see the *wind's power*,
the *rain's cleansing*
and the *sun's radiant life*,
one need only to look
at the horse.

"When your horse follows you
without being asked,
when he rubs his head on yours,
and when you look at him
and feel a tingle down your spine...
you know you are loved."

· John Lyons ·

A horse never runs so fast
as when he has other horses
to catch up and outpace.

⟋⟍ OVID

Saying goodbye is hard, even when you can't be there to say it. Wish I could have been there yesterday to say goodbye to this ol' guy. But he knows that I would have told him how handsome he was, gathered his forelock in my hand, and hugged him around his neck like a six-year-old; and I know that he would have pulled away (as if to roll his eyes at me), the way he always did. After almost three decades, we had an understanding. He knew that as of late he would only see me when I needed a certain kind of soul food; and I knew that he would deliver on my whim. He knew that we would predictably go racing across the hayfield; and I knew that he would let out a few bucks when he got to feeling good. He knew that, wind in my hair and smile on my face, it would make me laugh out loud. I knew that he would stop dead in his tracks at the top of each hill; and he knew that I would ask him to do it all over again. *Soul food.*

We both knew these rides were numbered. He knew that yesterday was his day to ride away; and I knew that it would hurt like hell to see him go. I hope he runs like the wind, hears my laughter in the breeze, and then does it all over again. ⁓ NDF

"A stubborn horse
will walk *behind* you.
An impatient horse
will walk *in front* of you.
A noble companion
will walk *beside* you."

AUTHOR UNKNOWN

Evening Listening

There is different relaxation
about watching horses while they eat.

There's a calm in the corral that can't be found
in the everyday hustle of the workaday world.
Listening to the sound of horses methodically chewing,
with an occasional swish of a tail.

Listening to the soft rustle of hay as the horses
toss it about, finding all the good bits. Horses deeply
contented, broken only by the occasional posturing
of a mare. A pinned ear; a sour glance—
all while the sweet smell of hay beckons.

There is a feeling of well-being and abundance.

"Lover *of* Horses"

My given name is Phillip, which literally means "lover of horses." Although I am not positive, my parents probably gave me that name because they simply liked the sound of it, and since I did not grow up around animals, I never dreamed that one day this would be part of how I would describe myself.

As a father of four girls, living in a rural Wisconsin town, our family's journey with horses began when my wife wanted to do "a family thing." Little did we know that that one decision would steer us for the next twenty-five years—horses would become central to the life of our family.

Almost from the beginning, I was involved with the day-to-day needs with caring for the horses: feeding, grooming, exercising, and cleaning stalls. We soon found that some of our habits needing changing, replaced with new ones, centered around the horses.

To be greeted each morning and evening with the nicker of horses calling out, "Where's my food," was refreshing and uplifting. As big as horses are, they are still very fragile and need us to care for them. But, we need them too. I can't explain it, but all the stories I can tell involve a give-and-take relationship. For our girls, these relationships with the horses have helped shape their lives into who they are today.

When I first started with horses, I was watching some people during riding lessons, when I noticed an older man leaning up against a fence. I asked him, "Do you have a horse big enough for me to ride? I'm 6 foot 2, and weigh 200 pounds." Grinning, he took me to a stall and showed me a horse, one taller than I could see over. He then told me, "I will tell you this, if you start riding and jumping, it will be like a narcotic. You won't be able to quit."

Forty-five years later, with tears in my eyes, and a lump in my throat, I am reminiscing about how horses have impacted my life. And unbeknown to my parents, I became a true portrait of my name—*a lover of horses.*

PL

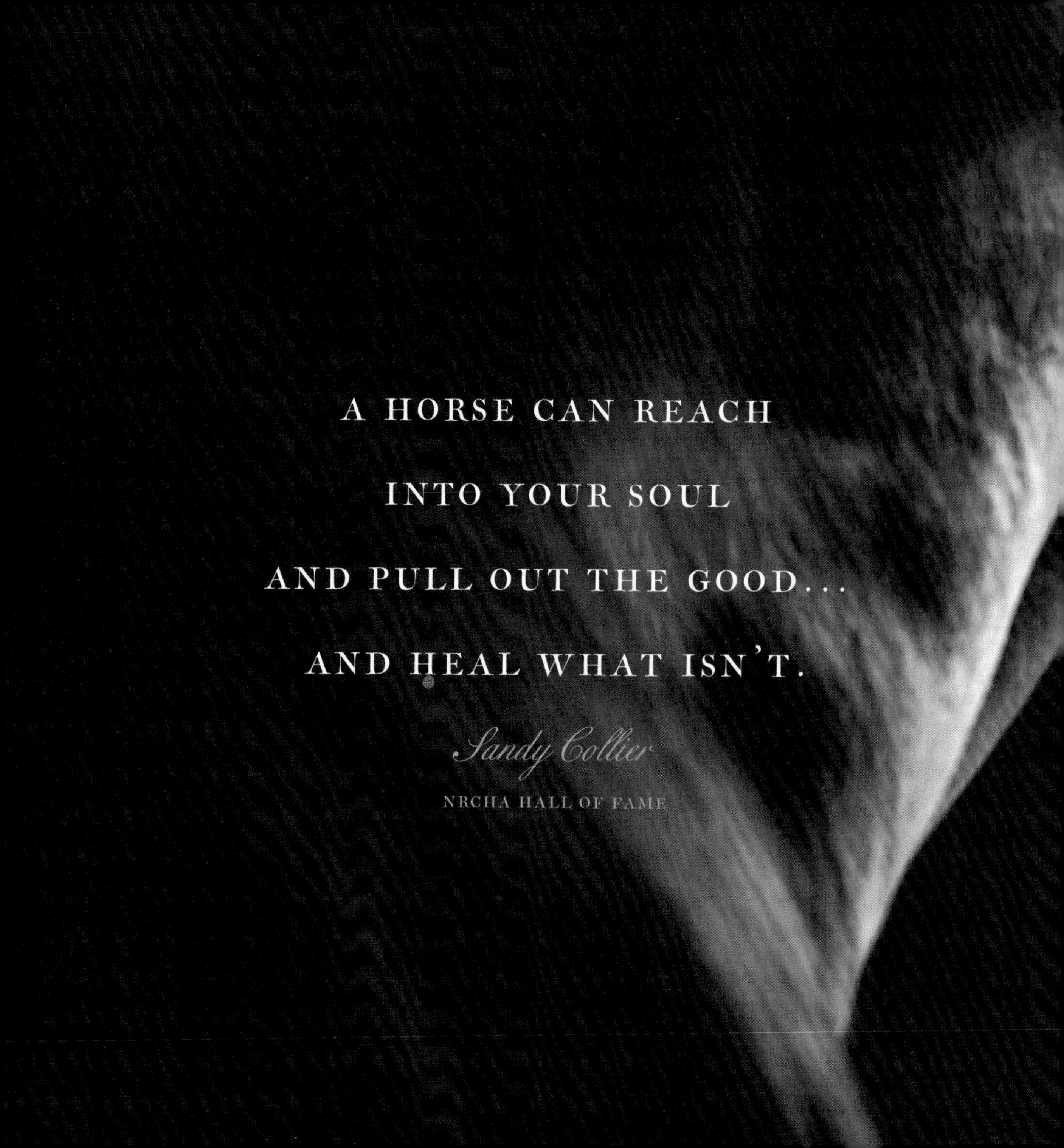

A HORSE CAN REACH

INTO YOUR SOUL

AND PULL OUT THE GOOD...

AND HEAL WHAT ISN'T.

Sandy Collier

NRCHA HALL OF FAME

FLIGHT WITHOUT WINGS

Our first horse, actually a pony, was a Grey Pony. But our second was a thoroughbred mare, retired from the track—we named her, Bownique, a beautiful horse, standing over sixteen hands high.

A very quiet, gentle spirit, I could put our five-year-old daughter on her without any concern of her misbehaving. But when I rode, she seemed to say, "I want to go, and I want to go *fast!*"

On our small farm there was a strip of grass between two fields about one-quarter mile long. On our frequent rides, we would always start at a slow canter. As I would rise up out of the saddle, she would sense that she could go faster. Then as I moved the reins toward her head and up her neck, with my body moving forward, she would move with more excitement. I could feel her muscular body and legs move beneath me. With her nose flaring and ears pointed forward, she was just waiting for me to say, "Go girl!" Then she was free.

We were both free—the wind blowing past my face, her mane blowing back toward me, and I could feel the power of a twelve-hundred-pound animal flying across the grass—exhilarating!

Today, forty-five years later, I still remember with vivid detail those rides and feel the same sense of excitement of being one with this beautiful creature. Just me and a mare—flying without wings.

"All horses deserve,

at least once in their lives,

to be loved

by a little girl."

· Author Unknown ·

Tack in the morning.
*Not a better smell
on earth!*

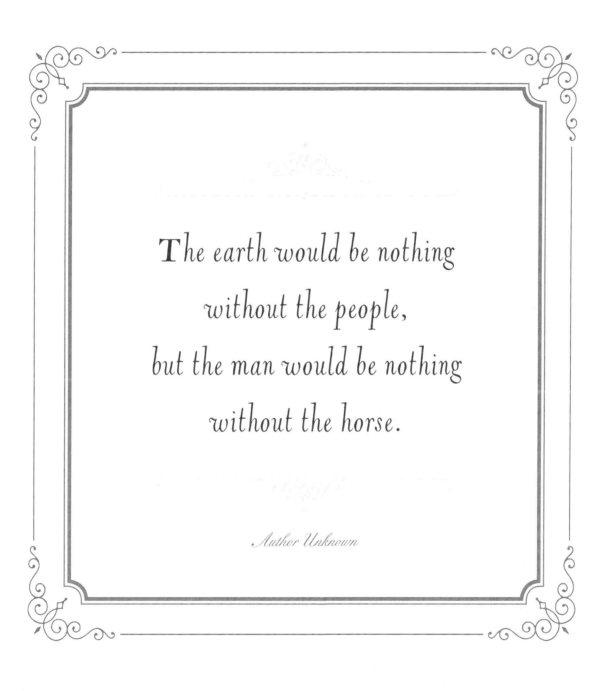

The earth would be nothing
without the people,
but the man would be nothing
without the horse.

Author Unknown

Farriers do the same thing every day.

Each day is different—different horse, different hoof,

and a different set of circumstances.

Successful farriers learn to understand the horse.

They listen to the whinnies, nickers, snorts, and blows,

as well as hoof noises, like pawing and stomping.

Although it's not their job to train horses,

a farrier needs to be the preverbial "horse whisperer."

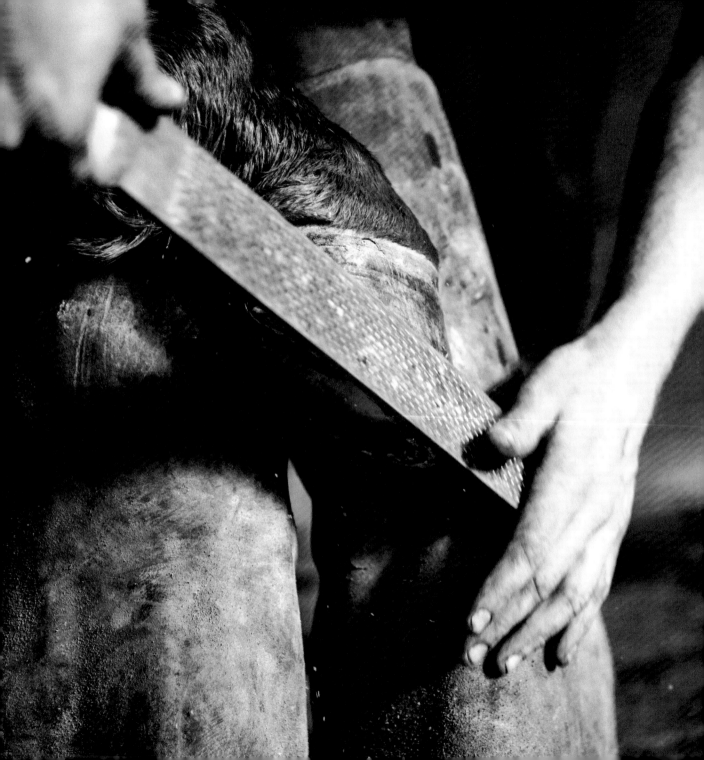

I have spent most of my life
riding horses.
The rest I've just wasted.

AUTHOR UNKNOWN

"When you look into a horse's eyes,
there is no judgment.
There is no prejudice.
Only freedom…
and 'Let's go have some fun!'"

Funny how the ones
that talk the *least*
are the ones
you know the *best*.

LOST!
Little Girl's Cat

Benji

We carefully painted these words on a 4x8 sheet of plywood and posted the giant sign on the corner of our property. It could be seen by anyone coming to the country intersection where we lived in a fifty-year-old farmhouse with our only daughter, who was four. "Benji" had been missing for three days, and we just knew that someone had stopped and picked him up from the corner field where he loved to hunt for mice.

The sign had its intended effect, because we soon received a telephone call from the guilty party. A woman's voice on the other end of the line gave a somewhat lengthy explanation of how it had happened that Benji got in her car, was taken away, and had since disappeared again! Disappointed, we gathered the details from the contrite neighbor, Joan, who had been so concerned about our sweet Siamese cat that she offered him shelter in her car. It seemed a nice gesture, but she was on her way to the fair in Elkhorn, twenty-five miles away!

Joan and her husband, Ron, raised Standardbred trotters, which they raced around the state, and were currently showing at the Elkhorn County Fair. Their beautifully moving horses won many ribbons and were valuable animals, particularly one black stallion. Ron and Joan took Benji to the show barn at the fair, intending to keep him in a stall and bring him back later in the day to find his owners. If you know anything about cats, though, you know you can't confine them to a stall or anywhere in a barn like that! Benji escaped, leaving no trace and no witnesses. They explained that they were sorry and that they would make it up to Julie, Benji's young owner.

In the meantime, we placed an ad in the Elkhorn paper looking for our lost Siamese cat. We received and followed up on several leads, none of which turned out to be our sweet pet. We stopped driving to Elkhorn with the hopes of finding Benji and decided instead to believe that he had found a lovely home with folks who adored him.

Meanwhile, Joan and Ron called and invited us to come over and visit their horse farm. The following Sunday, we went over to see them and met many of their horses, including the beautiful champion trotter, Midnight. Julie fell in love with the animals and had no fear as she reached up to pet them and look them in the face. Then we were introduced to Silver, a cute little white pony, which was the farm pet and looked to be a perfect fit for a four-year-old! Julie was in heaven when Joan offered us Silver and we accepted on the spot! That instant our lives changed incredibly as we took up the life of horse owners, a consuming hobby in which we were immersed for nearly thirty years.

It was a whirlwind of activity as we put up fencing, found some equipment, and located hay. True to his word, the trailer arrived two days later, and Ron delivered not only little white Silver, but her yearling foal Dusty. Taller than her mother, Dusty was a dark gray filly with fine conformation, an Arab dished face, and she moved with a floating trot! It seems that Midnight and Silver had accidentally produced this delightful pony, and she had just become ours. She was one in a million, as she turned out to be an extraordinary show pony and jumper.

Over the next few years Dusty grew into her gorgeous trot, and Julie grew into a capable rider and trainer as they went from 4-H to Open Shows to the A-circuit! Silver and Dusty stayed with us for many happy years, but they were only the first of many horses and ponies that joined our little family farm where Julie and her sisters grew up.

Every once in a while, I look out into that corner field where the ponies and horses lived and grazed, and I remember how Benji unwittingly introduced us to the horse life and the incredible joys and opportunities that our graceful and spirited animals have provided us for a lifetime! ⌁ ML

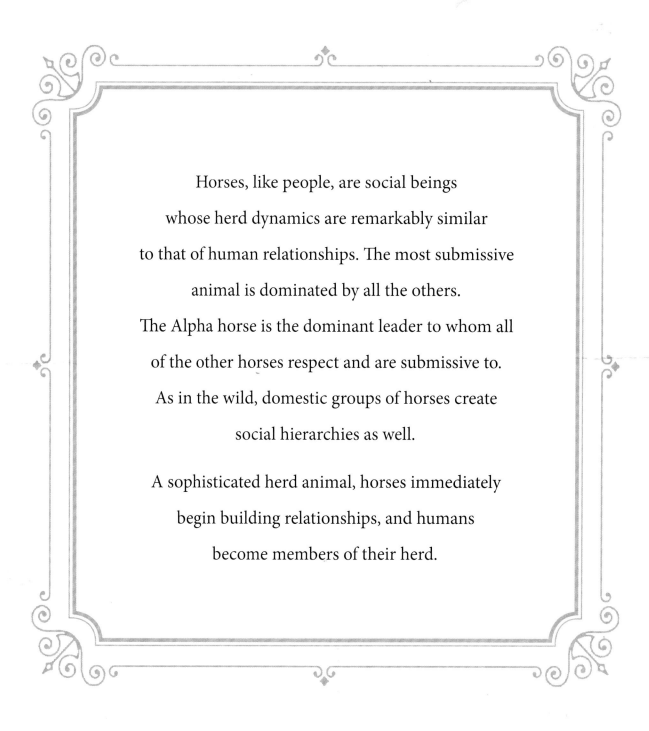

Horses, like people, are social beings
whose herd dynamics are remarkably similar
to that of human relationships. The most submissive
animal is dominated by all the others.
The Alpha horse is the dominant leader to whom all
of the other horses respect and are submissive to.
As in the wild, domestic groups of horses create
social hierarchies as well.

A sophisticated herd animal, horses immediately
begin building relationships, and humans
become members of their herd.

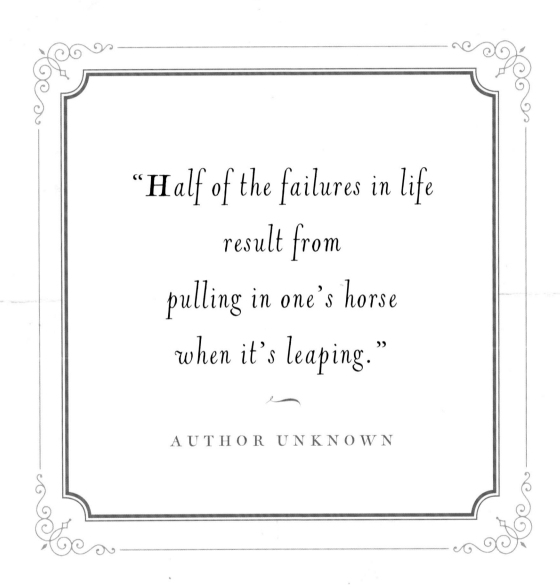

"Half of the failures in life
result from
pulling in one's horse
when it's leaping."

AUTHOR UNKNOWN

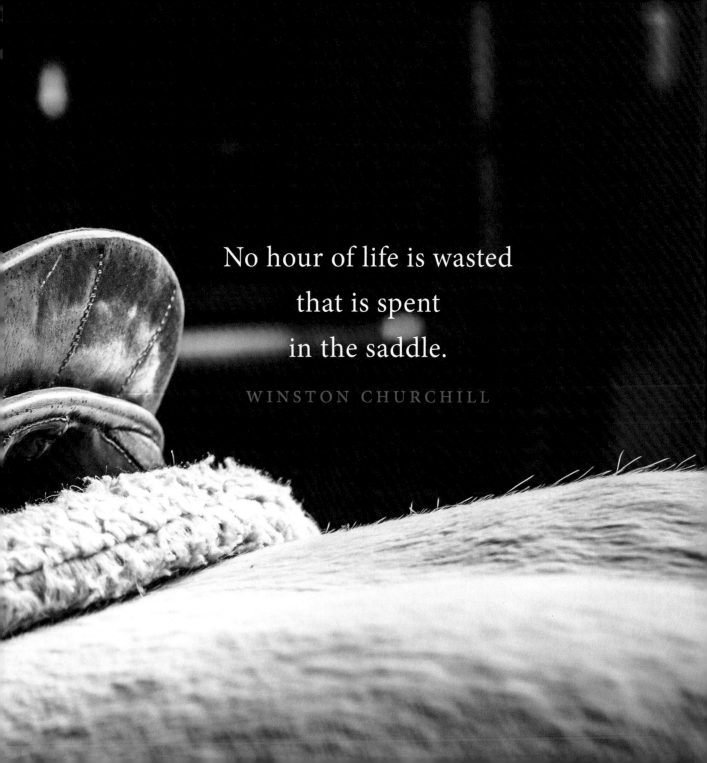

No hour of life is wasted
that is spent
in the saddle.

WINSTON CHURCHILL

I HAVE SEEN THINGS SO BEAUTIFUL

THEY HAVE BROUGHT TEARS TO MY EYES.

YET NONE OF THEM CAN MATCH

THE GRACEFULNESS AND BEAUTY

OF A HORSE RUNNING FREE.

AUTHOR UNKNOWN

American Horse

© 2018 KPT Publishing, LLC
Written by D. A. Michaels

Published by KPT Publishing
Minneapolis, Minnesota 55406
www.KPTPublishing.com

ISBN 978-1-944833-47-3

Designed by AbelerDesign.com

First printing November 2018

10 9 8 7 6 5 4 3 2

Printed in the United States of America